Don't be Fooled

Contents

Halley Court, Jordan Hill, Oxford, OX2 8EJ
a division of Harcourt Education Ltd

www.myprimary.co.uk

Help and support for teachers, plus the widest range of education solutions

Rigby is a registered trademark of Harcourt Education Ltd

Don't be Fooled first published 2004

Series editor: Shirley Bickler

08 07 06 05 04

10 9 8 7 6 5 4 3 2

Don't be Fooled
ISBN 0433 035110

Group reading pack with teaching notes
ISBN 0433 03565X

Illustrated by Alan Clarke, Hannah Thomson and Jennifer Ward

Cover illustration © John Haslam

Designed by StoreyBooks

Repro by Digital Imaging, Glasgow

Printed and bound in Spain by Edelvives

Kidnapped

written by Elizabeth Hawkins

illustrated by Alan Clarke

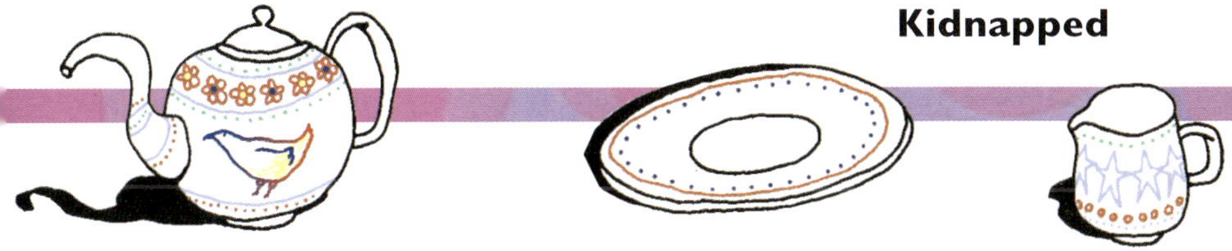

My Grandma has a china stall in the market. One Saturday, my big sister Daisy and I went to help Grandma. "I've a surprise for you," said Grandma.

In the car park was a new white van. "It's to carry all my plates and mugs and teapots," she said.

Grandma proudly showed us the new town plan. There were adverts around the edge. She pointed to one advert: 'Visit GRANDMA'S CHINA in the market. Finest china for the home.'

"Wow, Grandma!" I said. "You're going to be rich."

"You be careful with that van," said Bill Blundell. He has the stall next to Grandma's. He's got long greasy hair and dirty hands, and he sells old radios. "That's a fine van. A lot of people would like that." He winked at me and rubbed his stubbly chin.

I didn't like the way he talked. I was surprised Grandma trusted him.

We had a busy morning on Grandma's stall. I was serving a smart young man in a brown leather jacket.

"I'll have two of those robin mugs for my nieces," he said.

"That's the last one here," said Grandma. "But there's more in my van."

"We'll fetch them," offered Daisy.

"Look after the van key," said Grandma. "And, bring my mobile phone. I left it in the back of the van."

"Shouldn't leave valuables in the van," said Bill Blundell, as we ran past his stall. "It's asking for it."

"Asking for what?" I thought. I didn't know why Grandma was so friendly with Bill Blundell. He wore a dirty old jacket and never smiled.

We unlocked the back of the van. The wind was blowing hard. "Leave the key in the lock," I said to Daisy, "so we don't lose it."

We were unpacking the robin mugs when a gust of wind rocked the van.

"Watch out!" I cried, but the back doors slammed shut.

It was dark in the van, and freezing cold. We couldn't open the door. "Grandma will come and look for us," I said.

Soon the key rattled in the lock. But Grandma didn't open the door. Then we heard the driver's door open. Seconds later, the engine roared.

"I … I think the van is being stolen!" whispered Daisy.

"I bet it's Bill Blundell," I said. "He knew we had the key to the van."

"Where's he taking us?" cried Daisy softly.

The crumpled town plan was in my pocket. "I've got Grandma's map," I said. There was a chink of light round the bottom of the door.

I peered at the plan.

The van swung right, out of the car park. "Must be Silk Lane," I whispered. The van slowed to a stop, its engine running. "Traffic lights! Could be the junction with Endover Road."

Soon the van chugged uphill. "Castle Hill!" I guessed.

"I've found Grandma's mobile," squealed Daisy. "Where is number nine?"

Daisy dialled 999. "Help! Our Grandma's van has been stolen. We're inside. We've been kidnapped. No ... I don't know the registration number. I don't know where we are. We can't see out."

I grabbed the phone. "We've just driven up Castle Hill ... we're going over some bumpy ground now. Bill Blundell has stolen the van."

The van stopped. The driver slammed his door. I heard his footsteps crunch as he came round to the back. Would the police reach us before Bill Blundell opened the van doors?

Then I heard a siren and the screech of brakes. There was shouting. The police opened the back doors. Handcuffed to a policeman, was a young man. He wore a smart leather jacket, not a dirty old jacket. He wasn’t Bill Blundell.

It was the young man who had wanted the robin mugs. “I was only after the van,” he whined. “I was going to dump the kids …”

Grandma drove up in Bill Blundell's rusty old Ford.

"All right then, son?" Bill Blundell said to me. I felt bad. I didn't look at him.

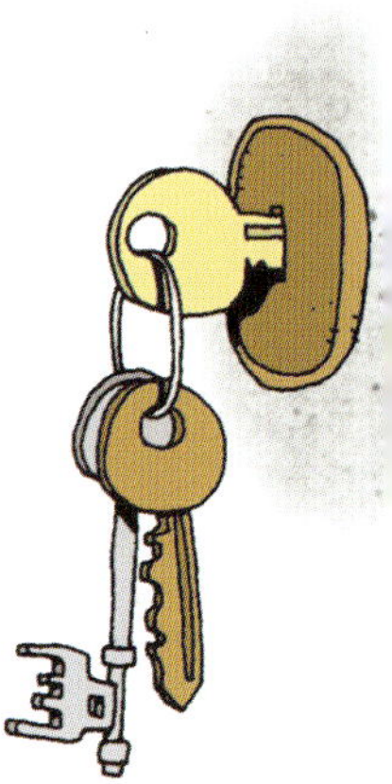

That was the most frightening day ever, but I learnt two things.

1. Don't leave keys in locks.
2. You can't tell a man by his jacket or his car.

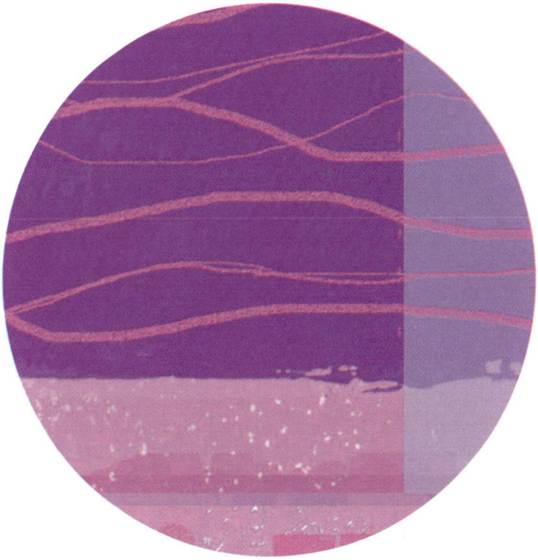

A Lucky Escape

written by Julia Jarman

illustrated by Hannah Thomson

Rik stood in the school doorway. Where was Tarik? He'd promised to wait, so they could walk home together to Tarik's house. Tarik had a new Playstation and a new game.

Amy saw Rik waiting. She said, "If you're looking for Tarik, he's gone – with Matt. Look! There they are! If you run you'll catch them."

It was getting dark. Rik could only just see Matt and Tarik – at the end of the road. He yelled, "Wait, will you!" But then some cars went by. When he looked next, they had vanished.

Luckily, he was a good runner and soon reached the corner. There they were, nearly at the next corner. He yelled again. They glanced back and then started running again. They wanted to get home first and start on the Playstation without him.

Rik speeded up, but then he got a stitch in his side and had to stop. Matt and Tarik disappeared again – and a car drew up.

"Want a lift, Rik?" A man was leaning out of the window. "You'll get wet if you stay out there," he said with a friendly smile. He looked a bit like Matt's dad. Was it him? Rik thought he'd seen him before.

"You live in Tylers Close, don't you?" the man went on.

Rik nodded.

"Get in then. It's on my way home."

It had started raining and the car was really cool, a Jag, the latest S-Type.

"You remember me, don't you?" the man went on. "And Bonzo here?" He pointed to a dog in the back. "You and your dad stopped for a chat the other day."

Rik did remember seeing him once before, in the woods. Bonzo had brought him a stick, and he had thrown it for him.

The man grinned. "And were they your so-called mates, running off without you? What would they say if you drove past them in a Jag?" He opened the passenger door. "Come on. Get inside. We'll show them."

Rik pictured Tarik's face and Matt's – going green as he sailed past. They'd been really mean to go off without him. And it would be good to get out of the rain.

"Come on. Get in. Let's wipe the smiles off their faces," said the man. "Get in the back if you like. I'll take you home."

Rik started to open the back door.

"That's right." The man closed the front door. "Bonzo doesn't bite – and nor do I."

He laughed – and something made Rik hesitate.

"We won't harm you, will we, Bonzo." The man leaned over and stroked the dog.

Suddenly Rik slammed the door shut and started to run, but as he did the man started up his car. Rik hoped he was going to drive away, but he didn't. He drove slowly by Rik's side with the window down.

"Don't be silly, Rik. Don't be silly."

Rik ran even faster, but the car kept up with him.

Then the car stopped. "Good," thought Rik. "He's turning round. He's going away."

But then he heard footsteps behind him. Oh no! The man was chasing him! Rik panicked. His heart was pounding. The footsteps behind him were getting closer.

Rik ran even faster, but then he stumbled and felt himself falling …

Everything went black. Then, fearfully, he opened his eyes – and found himself staring up at Tarik and Matt!

"Sorry, mate. We were hiding back there," said Tarik. "For a laugh. Didn't mean to scare you that much. Are you OK?"

"Y-yes," said Rik. "But ..." He saw the Jag disappearing into the distance.

"Cool car," said Matt. "Do you know that bloke?"

"Dunno," said Rik. "But he was weird. He tried to get me into his car."

"Better report him," said Matt. "Come on. Let's go back to your house."

"Quick!" urged Tarik.

The three of them set off at a run.

Back at home, Rik's mum rang the police. "They want to hear all about it," she said as she put the phone down. "They're coming round."

"You did the right thing, Rik," said his dad.

"We arrived just in time," said Matt.

"Yes," said Rik. "I think I had a lucky escape."

Too small for Football?

written by Haydn Middleton

illustrated by Jennifer Ward

Too small for Football?

Rashid finds out the hard way

Rashid only ever wanted to be a footballer. He was good enough to go all the way, but his team-mates sneered at him for being small. They made his life such a misery, he wondered if he should quit the game. "Am I really too small for football?" he asked himself.

Well, was he?

Rashid was football mad. He longed to be a footballer when he grew up.

"I think you love football more than you love me," said his mum.

Rashid smiled. "Only a bit more," he said.

When the family moved from Pakistan to England, Rashid was thrilled. England was where his all-time hero Michael Owen played!

In his first week in England Rashid went training at the local boys' club, Tiptown Tigers.

"You did well, Rashid," said Mr Price, the coach. "In Saturday's game, you and my son Dean can play as twin strikers."

"Twin strikers?" cried Dean. "But I'm twice as big as him!"

"So what?" said old Mr Burns, the assistant coach. "If a player's good enough, he's big enough."

The game on Saturday went badly and soon the Tigers were losing 3–0.

"Get the ball to Rashid!" yelled Mr Burns from the touchline.

"Can't!" Dean yelled back. "He's so small we can't see him!"

Moments later, Rashid won the ball in a tackle. Then he fired a lovely shot into the corner of the net. Goal!

"Yesss!!!" he cried. But Dean just turned away from him, and no one else in the team came up to say well done.

At training next week, Dean and the other players kept glancing at Rashid then winking at one another. When Rashid got home, he found an email from Mr Price. He stared at it, gobsmacked.

Rashid was badly shaken. He lay awake all night wondering how a coach could be so cruel. But first thing in the morning, Mr Price rang.

"I'm really sorry, Rashid," he said. "That email was from Dean, not me. I told him off and made it clear that you're the best player we've got. Anyway, you *are* playing on Saturday – OK?"

The Tigers lost their next three games. Dean and the rest of the team cared more about looking cool than playing well. None of them passed the ball to Rashid or spoke a word to him, and some of their mates stood watching behind the goal.

Whenever Rashid won the ball they chanted at him.

When Mr Price tried to stop them, they ignored him and chanted louder than ever.

During the third game, the abuse started to get to Rashid. He began to *feel* small and thin and useless.

Right at the end, his older sister Jamila came along. "Hey, Rashid!" she called. Her voice distracted him, and a big player barged him off the ball. Immediately a very loud chant went up: "He's small, he's weak, he's nothing but a freak!"

All of Rashid's team-mates sniggered.

"That was awful!" said Jamila, hugging Rashid after the game. "They're all horrible! You must leave this club right now!"

Old Mr Burns shook his head. "If Rashid walks away, then he'll be letting them win. You're a very good footballer, Rashid. I think you could be a great one. Don't let them stop you playing."

Rashid felt torn. He knew Mr Burns was right.

On the other hand, Jamila was right too. Those people *were* horrible. And Mr Price couldn't seem to do anything about them.

"So what are you going to do?" Jamila asked later on, at home.

"I'm trying to decide," sighed Rashid. "It's no fun playing for the Tigers. But I love football so much."

"Then play for someone else!"

"I can't. Other clubs are too far away. And please, Jam, don't tell Mum and Dad about this. They'd *make* me stop."

Rashid stayed away from training. That night, a note was pushed through his door.

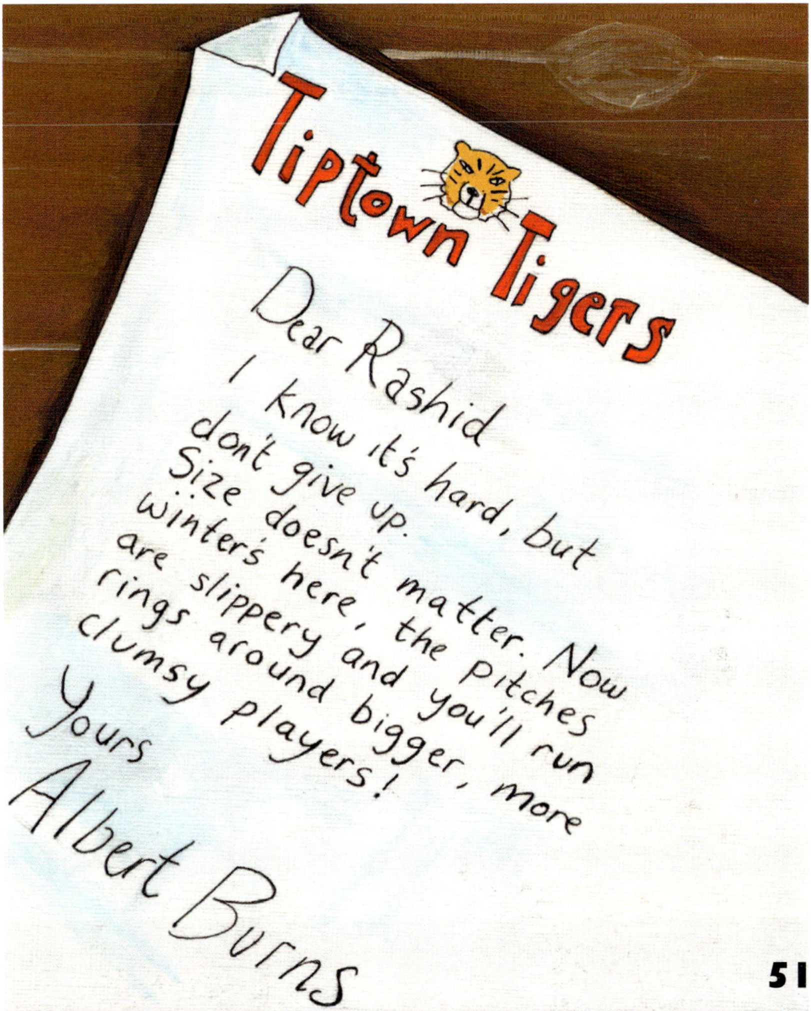

Without telling Jamila, Rashid played in the next match. Mr Burns stood next to the boys and managed to stop them chanting. And he had been right.

On the muddy pitch, Rashid kept skipping around the other team's defenders, but Dean missed two easy chances to score, so Tiptown could only draw 0–0.

Yet this was the Tigers' best result for months, and Dean led the team in a lap of honour. Or *almost* the whole team.

"Get lost, Maggot!" he snarled at Rashid. "There's something in your kit bag you should look at."

Back in the changing room, Rashid found a folded-up note:

Mr Burns grabbed the note from Rashid, screwed it up and threw it away. Rashid looked down with tears in his eyes.

"OK, son," said Mr Burns. "I've got a plan. Will you play one more game for the Tigers?"

Rashid shrugged. He was too upset to speak.

"One more game, Rashid. Leave the rest to me."

Rashid nearly didn't go to the game. He didn't think he could face it. Then he realised he couldn't let Mr Burns down.

When he arrived, the old guy just smiled at him. He said nothing about his plan.

It was raining so hard, all the boys stayed away. Most of the Tigers wished they had stayed away too, because the other team was awesome. But Rashid only ever wanted to play. If no one would pass to him, he would just have to win the ball for himself. So that's what he did – again and again and again.

Rashid ran, dribbled and shot like a demon. He even scored two goals – although the Tigers let in six at the other end.

A man with an umbrella was standing near Mr Burns. Rashid hardly noticed him. He was too busy putting every ounce of his energy and skill into the game.

"You were fantastic!" cried Mr Burns as Rashid left the pitch.

"Thanks," Rashid panted. "But what was your plan?"

"To get *me* to come and watch you," said a voice behind him.

Rashid turned to find the man with the umbrella.

"This is Mr Trevor Norton," Mr Burns explained. "He's a talent scout for Grimsdale in the Nationwide League. He thinks you're so good, he wants you to join his club's Academy!"

"*Really*?" gasped Rashid.

"Your parents have to agree, of course," said Mr Norton. "You'd start off in the Under-11 team. Then I think you'd stand a good chance of winning a football scholarship, and becoming a professional. How does that sound?"

"Pretty good," grinned Rashid.

"You've hit the big time, son!" said Mr Burns. "You're going to be the next Michael Owen!"

Seasons listings
Grimsdale Academy
Dear Rashid
Grimsdale Academy
Programme
Scholarship

Five months later ...

"Arsenal Academy 1, Grimsdale Academy 2"

And who jumped high to head the winning goal? Little Rashid!

"You were magic, Rashid," said Mr Norton. "Your team-mates think so too – they voted you Player of the Season. Now a reporter from the local paper wants to hear your story. Okay?"

"Okay?" laughed Rashid. "It's brilliant! Everything's *brilliant*!"

Too small for Football?

Rashid finds out the hard way

Young star says no way!

Rashid Abbas from Pakistan is the rising star of Grimsdale Academy. Yet five months ago he nearly quit football. At his first club they said he was too small to succeed, but one man disagreed – assistant coach Albert Burns.

Rashid takes up the story, 'Mr Burns kept telling me: If you're good enough, you're big enough. Now I hope I've proved that's true ...'